Try to Hunt, Tot!

By Sally Cowan

"You must hunt, Tot,"
said Big Jag.
"I will train you."

"Yes, Mum!" said Tot.
"I want to try!"

Tot could see some bugs.
She would try to get them.

She let out a big cry.

The bugs got a fright!
They went high up in the sky.

"You might have got a bug
if you had not yelled,"
called Big Jag.
"Try to hush."

A big green snake had a nap in the bright sunlight.

Tot jumped right at it.

“No, Tot!” said Big Jag.

“Why not?” said Tot.

"That snake will bite!"
said Big Jag.
"Let him lie there."

It was hot,
so Tot and Big Jag went
for a swim.

Bam!

Big Jag got a fish!
Her grip was tight.

Tot sighed.
She might be bad at hunting!

But just then,
she could see a moth fly by.

Wham!

"I got the moth!" yelled Tot.

"Oh my, Tot.
You are so quick!" said Big Jag.

CHECKING FOR MEANING

1. What did Tot try to catch first? *(Literal)*
2. Why did Big Jag tell Tot not to hunt the snake? *(Literal)*
3. How did Big Jag feel about Tot at the end of the story? How can you tell? *(Inferential)*

EXTENDING VOCABULARY

might	How many sounds are in the word *might*? Which letters make the long /ī/ sound? Which other words in the story rhyme with *might*?
hush	What does the word *hush* mean? What is another way the author could have written "*Try to hush*"?
lie	Say the word *lie*. If you replace the letter *l* with the letter *p*, what word do you make?

MOVING BEYOND THE TEXT

1. Tot learned to hunt from her mum, Big Jag. What would you like to learn to do?
2. What are some things you have already learned to do?
3. What skills do animals need to be good hunters?
4. Tot and Big Jag had a swim in the river when it got hot. How do you stay cool when it is hot?

TIME TO WRITE

Write about a time when you've had to learn a new skill. What did you learn and who helped you? How did you feel along the way?

PRACTICE WORDS

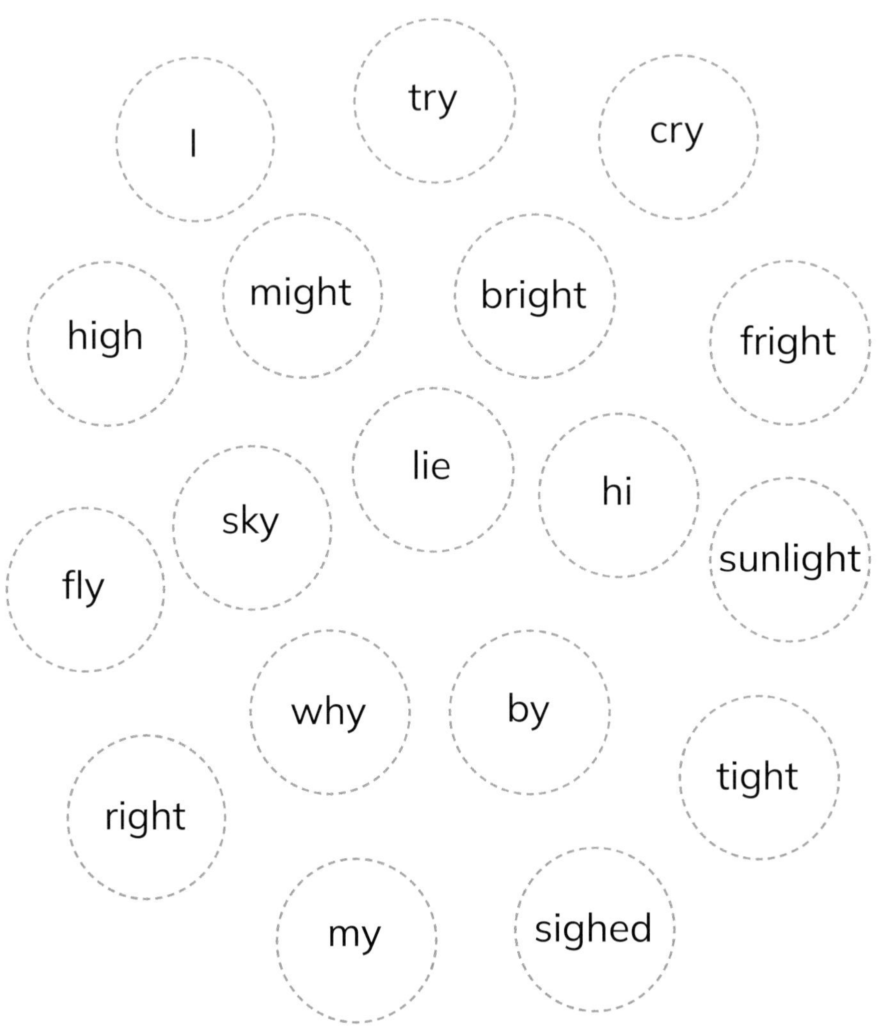